Music Legends

By Jeri Cipriano

GOSPEL SINGER

MAHALIA JACKSON

USA 32

1998

Scott Foresman
is an imprint of

Glenview, Illinois • Boston, Massachusetts • Chandler, Arizona •
Upper Saddle River, New Jersey

Photographs

Every effort has been made to secure permission and provide appropriate credit for photographic material. The publisher deeply regrets any omission and pledges to correct errors called to its attention in subsequent editions.

Unless otherwise acknowledged, all photographs are the property of Pearson Education, Inc.

Photo locators denoted as follows: Top (T), Center (C), Bottom (B), Left (L), Right (R), Background (Bkgd)

ISBN 13: 978-0-328-47255-0
ISBN 10: 0-328-47255-7

7 8 9 10 V010 16 15 14 13

Singing was probably the first way humans made music. People sing to express all kinds of feelings. Singing is part of many kinds of worship too.

Gospel's First "Superstar"

Mahalia Jackson was a great American singer. Jackson was born in New Orleans in 1911. She grew up singing in church and listening to rhythm and blues music. One singer she liked was Bessie Smith. But Jackson had her own style. She was the "queen of gospel music."

Gospel music began in churches. When Jackson sang gospel, her strong, rich voice got people moving. She sang about hopes and fears—and about faith too.

When Jackson moved to Chicago in 1927, more and more people heard her sing. She started making records.

In 1963 Jackson sang to the largest crowd of her life. She sang on the steps of the Lincoln Memorial right before Dr. Martin Luther King Jr. gave his famous "I Have a Dream" speech.

Jackson won a music award called a Grammy. She was voted into the Rock and Roll Hall of Fame. In 1998 a U.S. stamp was created to honor her.

Bessie Smith Sings the Blues

Bessie Smith had a loud, powerful voice. Before singers used microphones, Smith's voice could carry farther than any other blues singer's voice.

Bessie Smith was born in Chattanooga, Tennessee, in 1894. In the 1920s, people called her the "Empress of the Blues."

When Smith sang the blues, she sang about the challenges African Americans faced. She made people feel the heartaches and joys in her own life.

People still listen to Mahalia Jackson and Bessie Smith today. Smith's powerful voice reminds them of life's ups and downs, and its sufferings and joys. And when they hear Jackson, they remember their own hopes, fears, and faith.